X GAMES

Skateboarding Vert

by Connie Colwell Miller

Reading Consultant:
Barbara J. Fox
Reading Specialist
North Carolina State University

Content Consultant:
Ben Hobson
Content Coordinator
Extreme Sports Channel
United Kingdom

Capstone
press

Mankato, Minnesota

Blazers is published by Capstone Press,
151 Good Counsel Drive, P.O. Box 669, Mankato, Minnesota 56002.
www.capstonepress.com

Library of Congress Cataloging-in-Publication Data
Miller, Connie Colwell, 1976–
    Skateboarding vert / by Connie Colwell Miller.
    p. cm.—(Blazers. X games.)
    Includes bibliographical references and index.
    ISBN-13: 978-1-4296-0109-2 (hardcover)
    ISBN-10: 1-4296-0109-4 (hardcover)
    1. Skateboarding—Juvenile literature. 2. ESPN X-Games—Juvenile
literature. I. Title. II. Series.
GV859.8.M56 2008
796.22—dc22   2007001742

Summary: Describes the sport of skateboarding vert, focusing on the X Games,
    including competitions and star athletes.

Essential content terms are bold and are defined at the bottom of the page where they first appear.

Editorial Credits
Mandy R. Robbins, editor; Bobbi J. Wyss, designer; Jo Miller, photo researcher

Photo Credits
AP/Wide World Photos/Chris Polk, 21; Jae C. Hong, 6, 7, 13, 20;
    Mark J. Terrill, 12
Corbis/NewSport/Matt A. Brown, 17; Steve Boyle, 8–9, 15, 26
Getty Images Inc./Ezra Shaw, 25; Jeff Gross, cover, 4–5, 27; Nick Laham, 10–11
MRZPHOTO, 14
Red Bull Photofiles/Christian Pondella, 22–23
SportsChrome Inc/Mike Ehrmann, 19
ZUMA Press/Martin Philbey, 28–29

1 2 3 4 5 6 12 11 10 09 08 07

Table Of Contents

Gnarly Gnar Jar

On August 3, 2006, fans swarmed a skateboard ramp in Los Angeles. **Sandro Dias** was beginning his X Games vert run.

Sandro Dias (SAHN-droh DEE-uhs)—a vert skater from Brazil

Sandro Dias invented
the gnar jar.

Dias launched into a flip called a gnar jar 540. To land this flip, Dias slammed the tail of his board down on the edge of the ramp.

Dias finished with an ollie to fakie. This trick involves landing backward. The judges were impressed. Dias' exciting run earned him a gold medal.

Vert Basics

Vert skaters ride on a special ramp. Vert ramps have steep walls for skaters to catch big air. Some ramps also have pipes, rails, and other **obstacles**.

obstacle (OB-stuh-kuhl)—an object like a pipe or a railing that skaters do tricks off of

Steve Caballero

Skaters cruise back and forth between the walls of the ramp. They do tricks called **aerials** and pull off many other crazy stunts.

aerial (AIR-ee-uhl)—a trick a skater performs while soaring through the air

Andy Macdonald

Sergie Ventura

BLAZER FACT

The first vert skaters caught big air by skating up the sides of empty swimming pools.

Bob Burnquist

Judges rate skaters on their
style and the difficulty of tricks.
Skaters are also judged by how
much air they catch.

Competing in Vert

There are several rounds in vert competitions. Judges rate skaters from zero to 100. The highest and lowest ratings are thrown out. The other ratings are **averaged** to find the skater's final score.

average (AV-uh-rij)—the most common score; this score is found by adding all scores together and dividing by the total number of scores.

Tony Hawk

In the first round, each
skater takes two 45-second runs.
The top 10 skaters from the first
round move on to the next round.

BLAZER FACT

The first X Games were
held in 1995. Tony Hawk
won the skateboarding
vert competition.

Mathias Ringstrom

The top 10 skaters take three runs each in the final round. They pull out their most wicked tricks. The skater with the best overall score wins.

Bucky Lasek

Vert Ramps Diagram

wall

lip

Vert Records

Bob Burnquist is a vert legend. In 2001, he earned a score of 98 at the X Games. This is the highest skateboard vert score ever received.

BLAZER FACT

An event announcer cheered so loudly after Burnquist's 2001 run that he lost his voice.

Bob Burnquist

Other vert stars include Andy Macdonald, Shaun White, and Bucky Lasek. These skaters continue to invent fresh moves to impress their fans.

Andy Macdonald

Skateboarding vert is always changing. Fans can't wait to see what new tricks skaters will bust next. The excitement keeps fans coming back year after year.

Catching Some Air!

Glossary

aerial (AIR-ee-uhl)—a trick that is done in the air

average (AV-uh-rij)—the most common score; an average score is found by adding all scores together and dividing by the number of scores.

competition (kom-puh-TISH-uhn)—a contest between two or more people

invent (in-VENT)—to create a new thing or method

obstacle (OB-stuh-kuhl)—an object that skaters use when performing tricks

Read More

Crossingham, John, and Bobbie Kalman. *Extreme Skateboarding.* Extreme Sports No Limits! New York: Crabtree, 2004.

Higgins, Matt. *Insider's Guide to Action-Sports.* Sports Illustrated Kids. New York: Scholastic Reference, 2006.

Internet Sites

FactHound offers a safe, fun way to find Internet sites related to this book. All of the sites on FactHound have been researched by our staff.

Here's how:
1. Visit *www.facthound.com*
2. Choose your grade level.
3. Type in this special code **1429601094** for age-appropriate sites. You may also browse subjects by clicking on letters, or by clicking on pictures or words.
4. Click on the **Fetch It** button.

FactHound will fetch the best sites for you!

Index